Elliott, Lynne.
Clothing in the Middle Ages

1/07

The Medieval World

Clothing
in the Middle Ages

Lynne Elliott

Crabtree Publishing Company

www.crabtreebooks.com

Crabtree Publishing Company

www.crabtreebooks.com

Coordinating editor: Ellen Rodger

Project editor: Carrie Gleason

Designer and production coordinator: Rosie Gowsell

Scanning technician: Arlene Arch-Wilson

Prepress production: Samara Parent

Art director: Rob MacGregor

Project development, editing, photo editing, and layout:
First Folio Resource Group, Inc.: Tom Dart, Jaimie Nathan, Debbie Smith, Anikó Szocs

Photo research: Maria DeCambra

Consultant: Isabelle Cochelin, University of Toronto

Photographs: Alinari/Art Resource, NY: p. 30 (bottom); Archivo Iconografico, S.A./Corbis/magmaphoto.com: p. 23 (bottom left); Art Archive/Bibliothèque Municipale Rouen/Dagli Orti: p. 16; Art Archive/Bodleian Library Oxford/MS Auct. D. inf. 2.11. folio 8r: p. 8 (left); Art Archive/Musée Condé Chantilly/Dagli Orti: p. 8 (right), p. 20 (left); Art Archive/Musée des Arts Décoratifs Paris/Dagli Orti: p. 18 (bottom); Art Archive/Musée Thomas Dobrée Nantes/Dagli Orti: title page; Art Archive/Museo de Arte Antiga Lisbon/Dagli Orti: p. 23 (bottom right); Art Archive/ Neuschwanstein Castle Germany/Dagli Orti: cover; Art Archive/ San Alberto di Butrio Abbey Ponte Nizza/Dagli Orti: p. 26 (left); Art Archive/University Library Heidelberg/Dagli Orti: p. 18 (top); Art Archive/Victoria and Albert Museum London/Sally Chappell: p. 31 (right); Art Archive/Victoria and Albert Museum London/Eileen Tweedy: p. 25 (top); Courtesy of the Bata Shoe Museum, Toronto: p. 13 (top left), p. 13 (bottom left), p. 13 (bottom right); Bibliothèque de L'Arsenal, Paris, France/Archives Charmet/Bridgeman Art Library: p. 28 (left); British Library/ Add. 18750 f.3: p. 9 (left); British Library/Topham-HIP/The

Image Works: p. 10 (bottom right), p. 21, p. 25 (bottom right), p. 30 (top left); British Museum/Bridgeman Art Library: p. 24 (bottom left); British Museum/Topham-HIP/The Image Works: p. 11 (bottom right); Christie's Images/Corbis/magmaphoto.com: p. 31 (left); Glasgow University Library, Scotland/Bridgeman Art Library: p. 27; Christel Gerstenberg/Corbis/magmaphoto.com: p. 11 (left); Hamburg Kunsthalle, Hamburg, Germany/Bridgeman Art Library: p. 29 (left); Erich Lessing/Art Resource, NY: p. 10 (top right), p. 23 (top left), p. 30 (top right); Mary Evans Picture Library: p. 22 (right); National Gallery Collection, By kind permission of the Trustees of the National Gallery, London/ Corbis/magmaphoto.com: p. 22 (left); National Museums of Scotland/Bridgeman Art Library: p. 25 (bottom left); New York Public Library/Art Resource, NY: p. 19 (bottom); Réunion des Musées Nationaux/Art Resource, NY: p. 5 (bottom), p. 11 (top right); Heini Schneebeli/Bridgeman Art Library: p. 24 (top right); Science Museum/Topham/The Image Works: p. 24 (centre right); Singleton Open Air Museum, West Sussex, UK/Bridgeman Art Library: p. 28 (right); Stapleton Collection/Bridgeman Art Library: p. 19 (top); Aldo Tutino/Art Resource, NY: p. 24 (bottom right); Sandro Vannini/Corbis/magmaphoto.com: p. 26 (right)

Illustrations: Jeff Crosby: p. 7 (all), pp. 14–15; Katherine Kantor: flags, title page (border), copyright page (bottom), p. 20 (bottom); Margaret Amy Reiach: borders, gold boxes, title page (illuminated letter), copyright page (top), contents page (all), pp. 4-5 (timeline), p. 4 (top), p. 5 (top), p. 6 (all), p. 9 (bottom), p. 10 (left), p. 12 (all), p. 13 (right), p. 17 (bottom), p. 32 (all)

Cover: Noblewomen in the later Middle Ages wore clothing made of luxurious fabrics, elaborate headdresses, and beautiful jewelry.

Title page: Women spun wool into thread using spinning wheels.

Crabtree Publishing Company

www.crabtreebooks.com   1-800-387-7650

Cataloging-in-Publication Data
Elliott, Lynne.
  Clothing in the Middle Ages / Lynne Elliott.
    p. cm. -- (The medieval world)
Includes index.
  ISBN 0-7787-1351-2 (RLB) -- ISBN 0-7787-1383-0 (pbk)
  1. Clothing and dress--History--Medieval, 500-1500. 2.Civilization, Medieval. I. Title. II. Series.
  Medieval world (Crabtree Publishing Company)
  GT575.E55 2004
  391'.009'02--dc22
                                                    2004000804
                                                          LC

Published in
the United States
PMB 16A
350 Fifth Ave.,
Suite 3308
New York, NY

Published
in Canada
616 Welland Ave.,
St. Catharines,
Ontario, Canada
L2M 5V6

Published in the
United Kingdom
73 Lime Walk,
Headington,
Oxford
0X3 7AD
United Kingdom

Published
in Australia
386 Mt. Alexander Rd.,
Ascot Vale (Melbourne)
V1C 3032

Table of Contents

Clothing and the Middle Ages

The Middle Ages lasted from 500 A.D. to 1500 A.D. in western Europe. During this time, society was ruled by nobles, such as kings and great lords, who had a great deal of land, money, and power.

Nobles granted parcels of land, called manors, to less important lords and **knights**. In return, the nobles received military help and loyalty.

The less important nobles rented parts of their manors to farmers called peasants. As rent, the peasants gave the lord some of the crops they grew and animals they raised. They also worked in the lord's fields two to three days a week.

▶ *Kings and nobles at the top of society held all the power, while peasants at the bottom grew food and made material and clothing for themselves and the lords.*

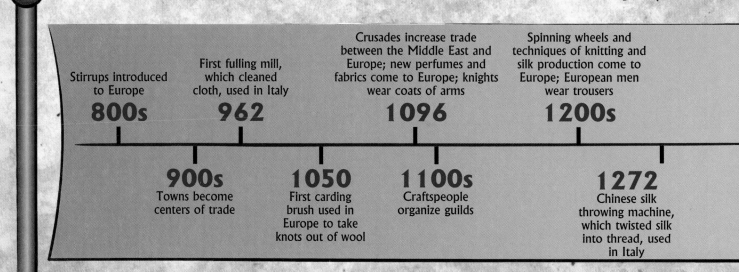

Stirrups introduced to Europe **800s**	First fulling mill, which cleaned cloth, used in Italy **962**	Crusades increase trade between the Middle East and Europe; new perfumes and fabrics come to Europe; knights wear coats of arms **1096**	Spinning wheels and techniques of knitting and silk production come to Europe; European men wear trousers **1200s**
900s Towns become centers of trade	**1050** First carding brush used in Europe to take knots out of wool	**1100s** Craftspeople organize guilds	**1272** Chinese silk throwing machine, which twisted silk into thread, used in Italy

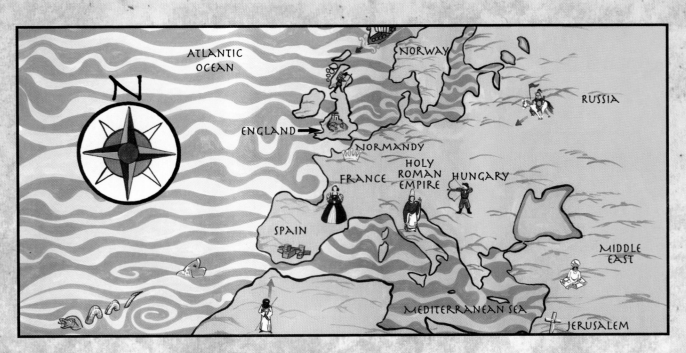

▲ *In the 1300s, European* merchants *began to trade more with merchants from Asia and the Middle East. The increased trade meant that wealthier townspeople and nobles in Europe could buy clothing made with beautiful fabrics from these faraway lands.*

Differences in Clothing

There were large differences in the clothing that nobles and peasants wore. For nobles, clothing was a sign of importance and power. They wore expensive outfits made of luxurious materials, such as silk and velvet. Peasants wore simple, inexpensive clothing that kept them warm and dry as they worked in the fields.

Clothing laws in the 1400s forbade people to dress like those considered more important than them. For example, **apprentices** in England who worked for expert craftspeople, called masters, could not dress like the masters. Townswomen in Florence, Italy could not wear striped gowns or fabrics **embroidered** with gold and silver because they might be mistaken for noblewomen.

▼ *Royalty and nobles wore expensive clothing that included fur-lined robes and felt hats.*

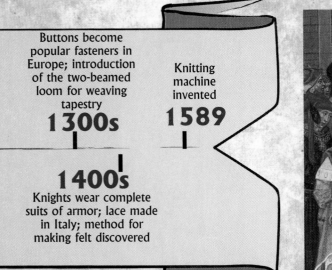

Buttons become popular fasteners in Europe; introduction of the two-beamed loom for weaving tapestry
1300s

Knitting machine invented
1589

1400s
Knights wear complete suits of armor; lace made in Italy; method for making felt discovered

Making Fabrics

People in the Middle Ages used linen, cotton, leather, fur, and silk to make clothing. These items came from various plants, animals, and insects. The most popular fabric was wool. For most of the Middle Ages, women in the countryside made woolen cloth by hand or with a few handheld tools. In the later Middle Ages, woolen cloth was made by craftspeople in towns.

▼ Linen was made from the stringy inner fibers of the flax plant. It was used to make shirts, bed sheets, undergarments, and towels.

▲ Fur came from the coats of animals such as squirrels, foxes, rabbits, and ermines. It was used to trim and line winter coats and robes, and was later mixed with wool to make felt hats.

▶ Cotton, which was brought to Europe from the Middle East and India, was made from fibers taken from the seed pods of the cotton plant. Cotton was used for light undergarments, summer clothing, bed sheets, veils, handkerchiefs, and light blankets.

◀ Leather was made from the hides of cattle, oxen, horses, and goats. It was used to make shoes, purses, belts, gloves, and holders for knives and swords.

▶ Silkworms produced strands of liquid that hardened into silk thread. The worms spun the thread into cocoons. The cocoons were soaked in boiling water to soften the thread, then the thread was woven into cloth. Silk was used to make beautiful robes, coats, and dresses for the very wealthy.

Making Wool in the Middle Ages

Shearing

In the spring, farmers and their wives used a type of scissors called shears to remove a sheep's wool, or fleece. They sold the fleece to wool merchants.

Cleaning and Carding

A wool merchant's assistants cleaned the dirt off the wool with warm water and soap. A carder combed knots out of the fleece with a card, which is like a hairbrush.

Spinning

The fuzzy wool was spun, or twisted into thread, using spinning wheels.

Weaving

A weaver wove thread into cloth on a machine called a loom.

Dyeing

A dyer and his assistants colored the cloth with dyes made from plants, vegetables, and tree bark.

Fulling

Fullers cleaned the cloth and made it thicker by trampling on it in a barrel full of sand and a chemical called lye. Later in the Middle Ages, cloth was fulled with hammers.

Napping and Trimming

Some cloth was napped, or brushed with a prickly plant, to make it softer, then the cloth's fibers were trimmed with shears.

Selling and Sewing Cloth

Drapers sold fabric to people who wanted to make their own clothing and to tailors who sewed clothes for customers.

Men's Clothing

The type of clothing that men wore and the quality of their clothing depended on how wealthy they were. Peasant men's clothing was made of rough wool dyed brown, green, or yellow. Wealthier men wore clothing made of a softer wool dyed in brighter colors.

Tunics

Men in the Middle Ages wore loose garments, called tunics, that were like short dresses reaching down to the knees. The tunics were tied at the waist with a rope or leather belt that held a knife in a pouch. Older and wealthier men wore tunics that were long and flowing. Linen undershirts kept the itchy wool away from their skin.

▶ In the Middle Ages, clothing was not designed specifically for children. Boys dressed just like their fathers. They wore woolen tunics and stockings, and leather belts and boots.

Stockings and Hose

Woolen stockings were like long socks that stopped above the knees. Hose were longer, going from the waist to the toes. Hose were held in place by a tightly pulled cord or by laces, called points, that attached to the tunic.

◀ Peasants often rolled down their stockings in the summer to keep cool.

Clothes for Work

Men in the Middle Ages wore clothes that suited their work, and they carried tools of their trade. Craftspeople wore belts on which hung large square bags of tools. Reeves were manor officials who carried tally sticks, which were wooden handles on which they kept track of the amount of crops and the number of days' work that peasants owed the lord. Jesters, who entertained nobles in their castles, wore colorful stockings, and tunics and hats with bells.

◀ *Craftspeople, such as blacksmiths, wore aprons while working to keep their clothes clean.*

A Change in Fashion

In the 1300s, styles changed for wealthier townspeople and nobles. Men's fashions changed the most. They began to wear hose with short jackets, called doublets, that ended just below the waist. Wealthier and older men also wore fancy robes, called houppelandes, which had high necks and long, flowing sleeves.

Kings' Clothing

Kings and queens were the most important nobles in medieval Europe. The clothing they wore at public celebrations, such as **coronations** and weddings, included crowns decorated with precious jewelry and fur-lined silk robes. Kings also carried two symbols of power: an orb, which is a globe with a cross on top, and a scepter, which is a long golden rod sometimes covered with jewels.

Women's Clothing

For most of the Middle Ages, peasant and noblewomen wore clothing that was similar in style, except that noblewomen's clothing was of better quality and was made of finer, more luxurious materials than peasants' clothing. Since noblewomen's clothing was so expensive, a good outfit was kept for a generation or two.

In the Middle Ages, women wore linen undergarments called kirtles or chemises. On top of kirtles, they wore tunics with long sleeves, and on top of tunics, they wore surcoats. A surcoat had open sides and no sleeves, so that the tunic's sleeves showed from underneath. Women also wore woolen stockings and belts with pouches for tools, coins, and other small items.

Peasant women wore simple tunics and aprons while doing farmwork. Peasants usually had only one or two pieces of clothing. Worn-out clothes were mended often, recycled into children's clothes and rags, or given to the very poor.

▲ Noble girls dressed like adult women in the Middle Ages, wearing beautiful gowns and veils.

Fancier Styles

Like men's clothing, the clothing of wealthier women became fancier in the 1300s. Some tunics had waistlines that came to just below the chest, while others were low and draping. Sleeves became more exaggerated, hanging to the ground. Women also wore houppelandes and clothing lined with fur.

Jewelry

For weddings, funerals, and other special occasions, noblewomen and men wore jewelry as a sign of their wealth and importance.

▲ Rings, necklaces, and bracelets were made of silver, gold, and semi-precious metals and stones. Popular jewels included sapphires, rubies, emeralds, diamonds, and pearls.

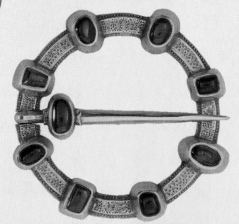

▲ Beautiful brooches and buckles held together nobles' robes, capes, and dresses before buttons were brought to Europe from China and the Middle East. Silversmiths and goldsmiths shaped the brooches and buckles into elaborate designs and filled them with precious jewels.

▲ Both noblewomen and men wore fancy belts, called knightly girdles, that hung slightly below the waist. The knightly girdles did not hold up clothing, but were just worn for decoration.

Hats and Shoes

In the Middle Ages, people wore hats for both work and fashion. Straw hats protected peasant men from the summer sun, while woolen hoods or caps, called capuchons, kept them warm in the winter. Craftsmen wore simple skullcaps, called coifs, or thin-brimmed hats to keep the hair out of their faces while they worked. Noblemen wore large, brimmed hats made of velvet or fur.

In the early Middle Ages, all women covered their heads with veils and linen wraps, called wimples. In the 1300s, wealthier women began to wear bigger and fancier headdresses.

▶ Capuchons had long pointed ends, called liripipes, that peasants used as scarfs.

▶ The "butterfly" headdress had a veil wired into the shape of butterfly wings.

◀ Wimples covered women's ears, necks, and chins.

◀ Fashionable women wore tall, cone-shaped headdresses called hennins or steeple hats because they looked like tall towers called steeples.

▶ Crispines, or crispinettes, were hairnets made of gold and silver cord.

▶ Some steeple hats had their points cut off to look like upside-down chimneys or flowerpots. These hats were called chimney pot hats.

Shoes

In the Middle Ages, people wore shoes and boots made of leather and cloth. Finer footwear was made of cordovan, a softer, more expensive type of leather from Cordoba, Spain. As the Middle Ages progressed, shoes and boots became fancier.

▶ Nobles who went horseback riding usually wore leather boots, called buskins. Buskins came up to the thigh and fastened with laces, buckles, or buttons.

▲ Men and women usually wore leather shoes or shoes made of cloth that fit close to the foot, like slippers.

▼ After 1400, long and pointed shoes, called poulaines or crakows, were fashionable. The length of a man's shoe was a sign of his importance. The longer his shoe, the more important he was. Poulaines went out of fashion quickly when people discovered they could not walk up stairs or even take a few steps without tripping over their feet.

▲ Pattens were wooden soles and leather straps that people wore with shoes and boots in rainy weather so that their footwear did not get muddy.

Clothing Trades

In the early Middle Ages, most people made their own fabrics and clothes. By the 900s, nobles and wealthier townspeople began to buy these items at weekly markets and at town stores.

Most shop owners were men who trained for years cutting, dyeing, and sewing fabric. Once they became masters, their wives, apprentices, and children worked with them learning the trade. Products were made by hand, with tools such as needles and thread, shears, knives, and measuring sticks.

1

2

3

Craftspeople

1 Shoemakers, called cordswainers, stitched together shoes and boots.

2 Hatmakers made hats, hoods, and headdresses using wool, fur, straw, and felt.

3 Tailors cut and sewed jackets, tunics, and doublets for wealthy customers.

4 Furriers sewed furs and fur-lined clothing for wealthy townspeople and nobles.

5 Linenmakers made sheets, blankets, pillowcases, tablecloths, and bed curtains.

6 Tanners prepared leather for shoes, purses, gloves, boots, belts, drinking mugs, and water pitchers.

Fabrics at Fairs

Fabrics that were not common in Europe were sold at large markets called fairs. These fairs were held throughout Europe several times a year. Some fairs lasted a few days, and others lasted several weeks.

Merchants came from all over Europe to buy and sell expensive European and foreign cloth. Then, they took the cloth back to their hometowns and sold it to local craftspeople.

Merchants also bought rare and expensive dyes at fairs. The dyes were made of plants, insects, and shellfish from the Middle East, India, and China. Bright red and brown dyes were made from the roots of the madder plant. Indigo, a brilliant color of purple and blue, came from the indigo plant. Henna, an orange-red dye, came from the henna plant. Crimson red, a color worn only by **emperors**, kings, and princes, was made from a crushed insect called the kermes beetle. Purple, an expensive and scarce color, came from shellfish in the Aegean Sea.

▼ *Fairs were busy, lively places where merchants bought and sold all sorts of goods, including fabrics, clothing, food, tools, and items made of leather.*

The Silk Road

To bring the foreign fabrics and dyes to European fairs, Chinese and **Arab** merchants traveled along a route known as the Silk Road. The Silk Road ran for 6,800 miles (11,000 kilometers) from China to Constantinople, now Istanbul, in Turkey. From there, Italian merchants shipped the fabric to the ports of Venice and Genoa.

▶ *Dyers colored cloth by mixing dyes in large, wooden barrels of water. Then, they stirred the cloth around with long poles until it absorbed the right amount of color.*

▼ *Traveling along the Silk Road (red line) was dangerous because of thieves, poor weather, and mountain, desert, and river crossings. The distance and danger made dyes and fabrics very expensive.*

Armor

Knights were medieval soldiers who fought on horseback with swords and lances. They wore special clothing, called armor, to protect them in battle. The suit of armor changed as weapons and ways of fighting changed.

In the 1000s, knights protected their backs and chests by wearing padded cotton jackets, called aketons, under chain mail tunics, called hauberks. Chain mail was made of thousands of small iron rings joined together. Chain mail hoods and cone-shaped helmets with nose bars protected knights' heads and necks. By the 1200s, hauberks were made longer to provide more protection, and knights wore heavier helmets with metal visors that covered their faces.

Plate Armor

Chain mail helped stop knives and swords, but it did not always protect against arrows. By the 1300s, knights wore pieces of steel plate armor on their chests and backs. By the 1400s, entire suits of plate armor covered their bodies.

Suits of plate armor had so many pieces that it took more than an hour to put them on. Knights needed the help of their squires, who were training to be knights, to get dressed.

▶ *Knights wore long linen shirts, called surcoats, over their armor to keep it from getting too hot in the sun.*

18

Heavy Armor

Suits of armor were very heavy, weighing about 50 pounds (23 kilograms). Sometimes, knights dressed in full armor had to be lifted onto their horses by wooden lifts, like modern cranes. If knights fell off their horses while fighting, they often could not get back up by themselves, and lay in danger of being killed by the enemy. Knights dressed in full armor who fell into deep water often drowned.

▶ *Special armor was made for a knight's warhorse, called a destrier. At first, the destrier's armor was made of chain mail and covered the horse's body and head. Later, when knights began to wear suits of armor, destriers wore plate armor too.*

Coats of Arms

Closed helmets and full armor made it difficult for knights to tell who was a friend and who was an enemy. To help them identify one another, knights began to wear designs, called coats of arms, that had specific patterns and colors. They wore the coats of arms on their surcoats, helmets, shields, and horses.

Coats of arms were decorated with patterns such as crosses, checkerboards, v-shapes called chevrons, and x-shapes called saltires. Animals, such as lions and eagles, and flowers, such as roses, were also popular on coats of arms. Each color on a coat of arms had a different meaning. For example, red meant bravery and courage, green symbolized youth and hope, orange was the color of strength, and purple represented royalty and high rank.

▶ *Men's coats of arms were in the shape of a shield, while women's coats of arms were diamond shaped.*

A Knight's Weapons

Knights used several weapons in battle, but their main weapons were swords. The finest swords were made out of iron or steel and were sometimes decorated with precious jewels. Knights also fought with lances, which were long spears made of wooden poles and iron tips.

If knights broke their swords or lances, they engaged in hand-to-hand fighting. They used daggers to stab enemies, maces, or heavy wooden clubs with spiky metal heads, to pound enemies, or large metal axes, called battle axes, to cut enemies in half.

One of the most important inventions for knights was the stirrup. Knights slipped their boots into stirrups, which attached to their saddles. This helped them stay on their horses while riding and fighting.

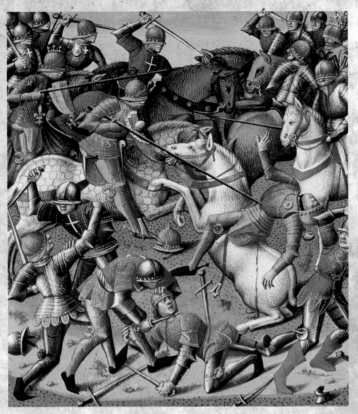

▲ *Knights used lances to knock enemies off their horses or to pierce enemies' chain mail. Shields were used to deflect enemies' sword blows and flying arrows, and to push enemies over.*

Foot Soldiers

Foot soldiers accompanied knights in battle. These soldiers, who fought on foot rather than on horseback, were usually townspeople or peasants. Some were paid to fight, while others were forced to fight without pay.

Many foot soldiers could not afford any armor, while others wore padded jackets, called jacks, made from many layers of quilted cotton. Iron chains or pads were attached to the jack's sleeves to stop swords from cutting through foot soldiers' arms. Simple iron helmets with visors protected foot soldiers' heads and faces, and iron gloves, called gauntlets, protected their hands.

▶ *Many foot soldiers had to provide their own weapons, so those with little money were poorly armed and protected.*

Archers

By 1300, archers were the most important warriors on the battlefield. They were trained to fight with bows and arrows. Some archers used longbows, whose strings were pulled back by hand, while others used crossbows, which required cranks. Crossbows took longer to reload than longbows, but arrows fired from crossbows pierced enemy knights and their horses more deeply.

▼ *Longbowmen and crossbowmen fired arrows from more than 100 yards (91 meters) away.*

Dressed for Prayer

In the Middle Ages, many men and women devoted their lives to Christianity. They wore distinctive clothing to help people recognize them as important members of the Roman Catholic Church, which was the only Christian Church in western Europe at the time.

◀ Priests

Priests were holy men who worked in neighborhood churches called parish churches. They led church services and performed **baptisms**, marriages, and funerals.

Priests were usually not wealthy men. Most wore simple woolen robes, but during church services they wore many layers of beautiful robes called vestments. The vestments included albs, which were long, belted tunics of white linen; dalmatics, which were long, unbelted surcoats worn on top of albs; and chasubles, which were ornate capes.

Bishops and Archbishops ▶

Bishops oversaw many churches in an area called a diocese. Archbishops were in charge of larger areas, called archdioceses, that were usually big cities. Not only were bishops and archbishops important religious leaders, they also played important roles in the government, helping kings make decisions.

Bishops wore the same type of garments as priests celebrating **Mass**, but they also wore large triangular hats, called mitres, to show their importance, and they carried crosiers, which were tall, hooked walking sticks that symbolized the bishop as a shepherd of his people.

Palliums covered archbishops' shoulders. These circular bands of white lamb's wool had long streamers and were decorated with five red and black crosses. Archbishops carried tall crosses covered in jewels instead of the bishop's crosier.

◄ The Pope

The pope is the leader of the Catholic Church. For much of the Middle Ages, he was a very powerful man in European politics, and he was very wealthy.

A medieval pope dressed mostly in red and white, colors that symbolize authority and purity. He wore a white linen robe, a red or white cloak called a papal mantle, red stockings, red shoes, and a red cape when outside. He also wore a small red cap, called a biretum, under his mitre, and a crown during processions and ceremonies.

Monks and Nuns ►▼

Monks and nuns were men and women who devoted themselves to prayer. Many of them also spent time studying and caring for people in need. They lived in communities, called monasteries, and convents that were set apart from the rest of the world.

Monks and nuns took a vow to live in **poverty**, so their clothes were usually simple and made from poor material. They wore habits, which were tunics made of rough, itchy wool dyed black, gray, or white. Over the habits, they wore scapulars, which were robes open at the sides. Monks sometimes wore cowls, or hoods, and they shaved the tops and bottoms of their heads, leaving a thin band of hair around the scalp, called a tonsure. Nuns always covered their heads with wimples and veils.

Clothing in Other Cultures

In the Middle Ages, people outside Europe wore clothing that suited their work or that showed their importance in society, as people in Europe did. The clothing was made from materials available locally. Wealthier people also wore jewelry made from minerals and stones from the region.

◀ *Aztec nobles, who lived in what is now central and southern Mexico, wore jewelry made of gold and stones such as turquoise and jade.*

▲ *West African craftspeople made gold pendants for kings and nobles. The pendants hung from necklaces and bracelets.*

▶ *From about age five, Chinese girls from noble families had their feet bound in cloth and wore shoes and boots that were too small so that their feet stayed tiny. Tiny feet were considered fashionable.*

◀ *Some Aboriginal peoples of North America wore moccasins made of deerskin. They also wore deerskin loincloths, shirts, leggings, boots, tunics, and skirts that were decorated with dye or embroidered with porcupine quills.*

Children's Dress

As in Europe, children around the world often dressed like their parents. Aztec boys wore strips of cloth around their waists and, if they were noble, finely decorated capes around their shoulders. Girls wore long, loose skirts and baggy, embroidered tunics woven from cactus fibers.

Young Japanese boys and girls wore kimonos, which were long wrap-over robes or tunics made from cotton, hemp, or silk if the children were nobles. The robes were belted at the waist by a sash. On the sash, boys and men wore boxes, called inro, to carry small items.

▲ Women in India wore long dresses made of elaborate silk fabrics, and jewelry, such as earrings, necklaces, and bracelets. Veils covered their long hair.

▼ Muslim men wore turbans and djubbas, long tunics with narrow sleeves. Muslim women wore veils and long robes, called ha'iks, that completely covered the body.

Hygiene

People in the Middle Ages had to work hard to keep clean. Few places had running water, garbage was often thrown into the streets, and diseases spread easily.

Handwashing was an important part of medieval life, especially before each meal, since people ate mostly with their hands. Wealthier people had pitchers of water, called ewers, brought to the table before and after dinner. Servants poured the water over the diners' hands and into bowls, then gave them towels to dry their hands. Peasants washed their own hands in bowls or pots.

◄ *Servants filled ewers with water that came from wells.*

▼ *Bathwater usually came from nearby wells or rivers.*

Bathing

Nobles who lived in castles had private bathtubs, which were barrels in their bedrooms. The barrels were placed near a fire that servants used to heat the bath water. In the summer, bathtubs were often moved to the garden. Bathtubs were made of wood, which caused bathers to get splinters. The invention of the cloth bath mat, placed in the tub, helped solve the splinter problem.

Baths in Villages and Towns

Peasants bathed in wooden barrels about once a month, and all family members used the same bath water. Baths were more frequent in the summer, when peasants bathed in nearby rivers and streams. Wealthier people in towns bathed more often. They paid to go to public bathhouses, where they washed themselves in large barrels and sat in steam rooms.

Soap and Shampoo

In the Middle Ages, most people washed with soap they made themselves. They mixed water with ashes, then boiled the mixture with animal fat. The soap cleaned well, but it was very rough on the skin and had an unpleasant odor. Nobles and wealthy townspeople used finer, more expensive soaps from Spain that were made of olive oil and herbs.

Shampoos were made by mixing olive oil, honey, herbs, and minerals. There were different shampoo recipes for cleaning hair, curing dandruff, making hair shiny and healthy, and hiding gray hair.

Using Steam to Bathe

In the Middle Ages, bathing in steam was a common way for people to get clean. Aztec people bathed in steam baths, which were small cabins with fireplaces that heated large stones. When the stones were hot, water was poured over them to create steam. As the bathers sweated, their bodies got rid of dirt and grease. North American Aboriginal men used sweat lodges, which were similar to Aztec steam baths, to cleanse the skin, but they also believed sweat lodges healed the sick and rid the body of evil spirits.

The **crusaders** brought the Turkish bath from Turkey to Europe. In a Turkish bath, bathers move from one room to another. The first room is a hot, dry room, like a sauna. The second room is filled with steam. In the third room, the bather receives a massage with oils. In the last room is a cold bath or shower. This series of baths is believed to cleanse a person completely and help relieve muscle soreness.

Getting Rid of Lice

Lice was a common problem in the Middle Ages. To get rid of lice, people made an ointment from **aloe**, a metal called lead, **incense**, and bacon with grease. They left the ointment in their hair for several hours. Then, they washed their hair with cleansing shampoo to remove the lice and the greasy ointment.

Keeping Teeth Clean

Toothpaste was made by mixing crushed barley, a metal called alum, and a bit of melted honey. People put the paste on their fingers or on twigs, which they used as toothbrushes. People also chewed on herbs, such as mint, cloves, anise, and fennel, to freshen their breath.

Toilets

Toilets, or latrines, were wooden seats or benches with holes in them. Chutes carried the contents of the latrines into **cesspits**, **moats**, rivers, or streams. Latrines were found in rooms called garderobes, or privy chambers, that were built into the sides of walls. At first, only castles and monasteries had garderobes, but by the later Middle Ages, many houses also had them.

People who did not have toilets at home used public toilets or chamber pots. Public toilets were built near town walls, rivers, and streams, and were available to anyone who lived nearby. Chamber pots were used inside the home. Their contents were emptied out the window as someone yelled out the warning "Gardy loo!" to the people below. "Gardy loo" comes from the French term *garde l'eau*, or "watch out for the water."

▼ *Some townspeople shared a latrine with their neighbors. This latrine was built between two houses, over a cesspit which was emptied a few times a year. Into the cesspit were dropped hay, straw, leaves, and rags, which were used as toilet paper. Wealthier people also used pieces of cloth.*

Beauty

In the Middle Ages, people thought that to be beautiful, women had to be slim, blonde, and fair skinned. They had to have white teeth, bright gray eyes, a large forehead, small lips, and a long neck.

High Foreheads

It became fashionable in the 1400s for noblewomen in Europe to have high foreheads, so they removed unwanted hair from their foreheads by plucking it, rubbing it off with a sharp **pumice** stone, or using a cream made of water and quicklime, a chemical that burns. They also trimmed their eyelashes and plucked their eyebrows thinly.

Hair Styles

Medieval women rarely left their hair long and flowing, unless they were unmarried girls, brides, or queens at their coronations. They usually braided their hair, sometimes making two braids that they wrapped around their ears and sometimes wearing one long braid down their backs. Women who wanted braids that almost touched the ground wore wigs and hair pieces made of human hair, flax, wool, cotton, and silk.

▶ *People in the Middle Ages brushed their hair with combs made from bone, ivory, or wood. Their hair was cut by family members, servants, and barbers, who also shaved men's beards, pulled teeth, and performed minor surgery.*

Men's Haircuts and Beards

Men's haircuts varied during the Middle Ages. Sometimes, men wore their hair long, while at other times, they cut it to chin length. By the 1400s, it was fashionable to have a shorter haircut, in a style now known as a bowl cut because it looked like the barber cut around a bowl placed on the man's head.

Young men and **clergy** in the Middle Ages usually shaved fairly frequently. Older men preferred to have beards. Some parted and waxed their beards into two or three points, or curled their beards by rolling them up when wet and then drying them during the night in bags called beard bags.

▼ *Perfumes and colognes were sold by apothecaries, spice merchants, and herbalists, or from merchants who went from town to town and from castle to castle.*

Makeup

Wealthy women in the Middle Ages wanted to look as pale as possible. They never tanned their skin, and some wore white makeup made of flour, chalk, or white incense, that was mixed with water or olive oil. Many powders contained lead, which poisoned the women who used them. Some women had barbers cut their arms and drain enough blood from their bodies so that their skin became pale. If women wanted the color of their lips to stand out from their pale skin, they put on lipstick made from the roots of vines or from seaweed mixed with **rosewater**.

◄ Women in Japan wanted pale skin, so they painted their faces white. Then, they reddened their pale cheeks, as well as their lips, with rouge.

Perfume and Cologne

Perfume became popular in Europe in the later Middle Ages. Noblewomen and wealthy townswomen wore perfumes made from the oil of plants, such as lavender, from flowers, such as roses and violets, and from herbs and spices, such as rosemary and cinnamon. Perfumes were also made from animal oils, such as deer musk.

Men also used perfumes on their bodies, in their bath water, and in the water they used to wash their hands before and after meals. Men's scents were made from lemon peel, nutmeg, cinnamon, cloves, and musk. Like women's perfumes, they were purchased from apothecaries, spice merchants, and herbalists, or made at home.

▼ Wealthy women in India lined their eyes with a black powder made of lead, called kohl. They also reddened their lips with beeswax and temporarily tattooed their hands and feet with a dye made from the leaves of the henna plant.

Glossary

aloe A plant with thick, fleshy, pointed leaves

apprentice A person learning a trade from someone more experienced

Arab A person from the Middle East or North Africa who speaks the Arabic language

baptism A ceremony that welcomes a person to the Christian Church

cesspit A pit for garbage or sewage

Christianity The religion that follows the teachings of God and his son on earth, Jesus Christ

clergy Priests or other religious leaders

coronation A ceremony to crown a king or queen

crusader A Christian soldier who fought against Muslims to recover the Holy Land, the area where Jesus Christ lived and died

embroidered Decorated with a design sewn in thread

emperor A ruler of a country or group of countries

herbalist A person who uses herbs to treat disease

incense A substance that is burned to create a pleasant smell

knight A medieval soldier, who fought on horseback, usually with a sword

Mass The main ceremony of the Roman Catholic Church

merchant A person who buys and sells goods

Middle East A region made up of southwestern Asia and northern Africa

mineral A naturally occurring, non-living substance obtained through mining

moat A deep ditch, often filled with water, around a fort that helps keep out invaders

poverty The condition of being poor

pumice A light, spongy stone

rosewater Water that has the scent of roses

Index

2 3 4 5 6 7 8 9 0   Printed in the U.S.A.   0 9 8 7 6 5